Evaluating Materials : Internal Evaluation of a sample Text Book

Introduction:

I0511337

Materials:

Anything which is used to help to teach language learners is called materials. Materials can be in the form of a textbook, a workbook, a cassette, a CD-Rom, a video, a photocopied handout, a newspaper, a paragraph written on a whiteboard; anything which presents or informs about the language being learned.

Materials Evaluation:

The systematic appraisal of the value of materials in relation to their objectives and to the objectives of the learners using them. Evaluation can be pre-use and therefore focused on predictions of potential value. It can be whilst-use and therefore focused on awareness and description of what the learners are actually doing whilst the materials are being used. And it can also be post-use and therefore focused on analysis of what happened as a result of using the materials.

In this presentation our evaluation is whilst-use and we have focused on awareness and description of what the learners are actually doing whilst the materials are being used.

Purpose:
The aim of this study is to evaluate the book "English For Today" of Class Three designed for general students of National Curriculum (Bengali Medium)

Age level of the student:
This book is marked for the students aged 9-10.

Proficiency Level:
They can write alphabets, memorize words & sentences, make simple sentences but cannot write paragraph of even 4-5 sentences by their own. Though they can read texts, can write but they can't speak.

Contexts:
This book is designed as a compulsory text for the general learners of National Curriculum (Bengali Medium).

Presentation & Organization of Units & Lesson:

There are units consisting of 48 lessons. 9-10 months will be required to cover all the units & lessons of this book.

The author's view on language & methodology:

The chairman of National Curriculum & Textbook board believes that to make teaching & learning English most effective particularly at the primary stage, in future this text book needs to be complemented with audio-visual materials. We observed some classes of two classes but couldn't find the use of any audio-visual materials.

Application of the materials is either as main core course or as supplement:

This book is used as a main course book.

Printing quality & Availability:

Locally available & it is supplied by the Govt. free of cost.

Availability of Vocabulary list or Index:

There is no vocabulary list or index in this text book.

Visual materials which the book contents:

The cover page of this book is not so attractive for the children of this age. Here more colorful & relevant picture would be included. Inside the lessons, topic related pictures have been included such as at page-7.
Here is a poem named Tea-pot & here an image of tea-pot is include which is relevant.
In page-37, there is a chart of name of 12 months.
In page-41, here also we find some relevant figures.

Recommendation:

The visual depictions are not that much clear. More colorful images could be included for attracting students. Quality of the binding of this book is low. Quality of paper used in this book is medium.

Cultural Biasness:

No cultural conflicts are there.

The Internal Evaluation:

We now continue to the next stage of our evaluation procedure by performing an in-depth investigation into this textbook.

- According to preface the 'English For Today' textbooks have been developed to help students attain competence in all four language skills in English through meaningful and enjoyable activities. It has been said that emphasis has been given on listening and speaking skills as the foundation on which to develop reading and writing skills. From the very beginning of this book we see that there are adequate tasks on listening, reading and writing. In page 6 we find that there is a lesson on dialogue. Students have been told to act out the dialogue. So task for developing speaking skill is also given. But the fact is that these tasks are not practiced in the classroom properly. What we have found by observing some classes and talking to students and teachers of different schools is that some very reputed schools students are given opportunity to practice these tasks. But in most of the schools these tasks are avoided. As for example, in BCSIR Laboratory High

School, task of page 4 that is writing on 'My Father' and task on introducing your mother have been totally avoided by the teachers. Another important fact is that students of Bengali medium in this level can say their father's, mother's name, but they cannot write passage in this stage. So it should be considered if this type of task should be included. The task of page 6 is also been avoided in most of the classes. So we can say that although four skills have been given emphasis into the book, it is not properly acquired by the students due to lack of practice inside the classroom.

- In Unit two there are lessons on the alphabet. Here students are told to read and write cursive letters which is not so important to include in this book. Students of this level are given hand writing book for practicing this type of tasks. And most of the students cannot write these letters properly. If we look at page 9 & 12 we find that the student from whom I have collected this book she couldn't write these letters properly although she is a good student as I know. So these types of tasks are not so necessary to make compulsory for this level of students.

- According to preface topics and themes have been selected in a way that would not only help students address the needs of real life situation, but would also inculcate humanistic values in them as well as broaden their mental horizon. Lessons of Unit-1 and Unit-3 which are about introducing myself & commands, instructions and requests have covered items to teach the students the needs of real life situation. And the lesson 3 of Unit-9 which is about the boys and the frog, lessons of Unit-11 which are about food and hygiene have covered the items to fulfill the other objective. In page 64 that is in lesson 3 of Unit-9 students are taught that what's play to one is death to others. So these things are really appreciable

- In this textbook Unit-4 is about counting numbers. Here too much emphasis is given on writing numbers which is totally unnecessary. Firstly, these are the things of mathematics, so these could be taught in that course. Here in English book these could be avoided. Or, one or two lessons would be enough for this purpose. Secondly, these types of lessons are included in the text book of class two. So here including so many lessons on these things is not only unnecessary but also repetition of the tasks of previous classes.

- Unit-5 of this book is also the repetition of the text book of class-two. Here lessons are of names of the days and months which are already taught in their previous class. So this item could be excluded.

- In Unit-7 students are given tasks to write short paragraphs. This item can improve students' writing skill. But as we said earlier students have to be practiced in the classroom more.

- And finally we can say that this book is not a self-study book. Students need proper guideline and help from their teacher to do the activities included in this text book. So proper teachers' training and classroom activities should be ensured to get the best use of this book.

There is a wide variety of reading and listening material available in this book but the speaking material is not very good and is too accuracy based. We have checked the table of contents and made a detailed inspection of several units. We would therefore have to add something in terms of reading and speaking fluency. The book is usable and could be adapted. On the whole the author's claims are realized in the materials. Consequently we can use this as a core course with some adaptations.

ENGLISH FOR TODAY
Class Three

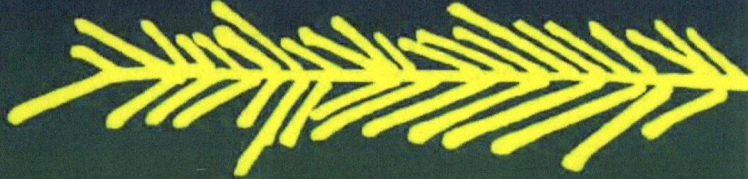

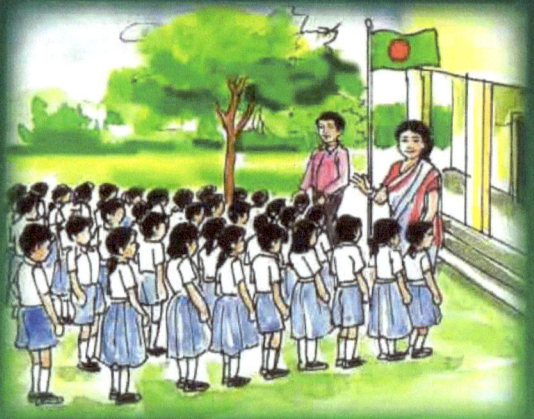

 NATIONAL CURRICULUM & TEXTBOOK BOARD, DHAKA

Prescribed by the National Curriculum & Textbook Board
as a Textbook for Class Three from the academic year 2013

ENGLISH FOR TODAY

Class Three

Writers & Editors

M S Hoque
Yasmin Banu
Md Abdur Razzaque
Naina Shahzadi

Illustrator
Prohlad Karmaker

Illustration Editor
Hashem Khan

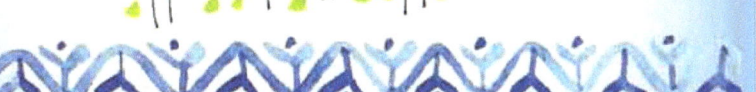

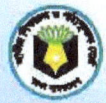

NATIONAL CURRICULUM & TEXTBOOK BOARD, DHAKA

Published by
National Curriculum & Textbook Board, Dhaka
69-70 Motijheel Commercial Area, Dhaka 1000

Trial Edition

First Edition: 2012

Coordinator
Abu Hena Mashukur Rahman

Graphics
Prohlad Karmaker

Design
National Curriculum & Textbook Board

তৃতীয় প্রাথমিক শিক্ষা উন্নয়ন কর্মসূচির আওতায় গণপ্রজাতন্ত্রী বাংলাদেশ সরকার কর্তৃক
বিনামূল্যে বিতরণের জন্য

Printed by:

Preface

The primary curriculum has been revised in the light of the National Education Policy 2010 which emphasizes learning English as an international language for communicating locally and globally. The 'English For Today' textbooks have been developed to help students attain competence in all four language skills in English through meaningful and enjoyable activities. Emphasis has been given on listening and speaking skills as the foundation on which to develop reading and writing skills. Topics and themes have been selected in a way that would not only help students address the needs of real life situations, but would also inculcate humanistic values in them as well as broaden their mental horizon. Grammar points and planned activities to develop students' competence in all four language skills have been presented within contexts in a systematic and graded way.

The 'English For Today' textbook is accompanied by a Teacher's Edition. However, we are aware that to make teaching and learning of English most effective and fruitful, particularly at the primary stage, the textbook needs to be complemented with audio-visual materials. We sincerely hope to do so in the near future.

My heartfelt gratitude goes to the curriculum developers, writers, illustrators and coordinator who worked under tremendous time constraint. But for their sincerity, commitment and hard work, it would not have been possible for the NCTB to develop the English textbook 'English For Today' make available to teachers and students all over the country by January 2013. As the book was developed within a very limited time, there is room for further development. Any constructive suggestions from anybody would help us improve the book.

I also sincerely thank all who have been involved with the production and publication of this textbook.

Professor Md. Mostafa Kamaluddin
Chairman
National Curriculum and Textbook Board
Dhaka

Contents

Start like this: My father's name is

....

....

....

....

....

D **Introduce your mother. Use the information as in C above. Work with a different partner.**

A Listen and recite.

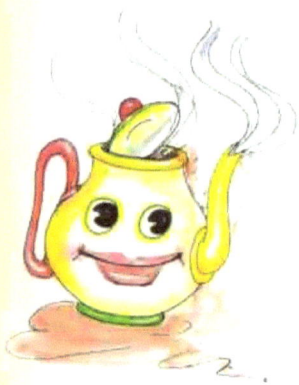

Tea-pot

I am a little tea-pot,

Short and stout.

This is my handle,

And this is my spout.

When the water's boiling,

Hear me shout:

"Just lift me up

And pour me out."

B Recite the rhyme yourself.

A Ask and answer.

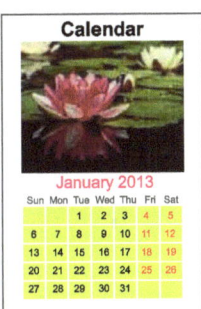

Q. What's this?
Ans. It's a calendar.
Q. What can we see in a calendar?
Ans. A month, days, dates and the year

B Look, listen and say.

January
February
March
April
May
June
July
August
September
October
November
December

Unit 6: People and occupation

Lesson 1: People

A Look, listen and say.

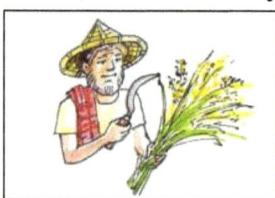

a farmer

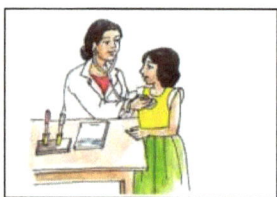

a doctor

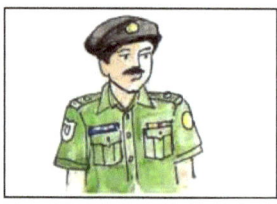

a policeman

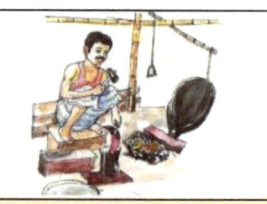

a blacksmith

A   Listen and read.

The boys and the frogs

Some frogs are croaking in a pond. Two boys are walking by the pond. They see the frogs. They start throwing stones at the frogs. They kill a frog and frighten some others. The boys are laughing.

An old frog raises its head and says angrily, "Stop! Stop throwing stones at us. What's play to you is death to us."

B   Match pictures with words.

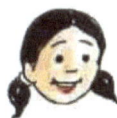   sad

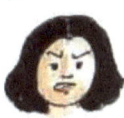   happy

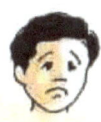   angry

A Listen and read the passage aloud.

We should eat good food. We get good foods from plants and trees. We get good foods from animals too. Rice, vegetables, fish, eggs, milk, etc are good foods. These are good for health.

But we should not eat ice-cream, chocolates, chips, burgers, etc. These are not good for health.

B Read the passage silently and answer the following questions.

1 What food should we eat?
2 Why should we eat them?
3 What foods are not good for health?
4 Why should we not eat them?

C What are your favourite foods?

D Listen and say.

fish   wash   plants   chips

A Read.

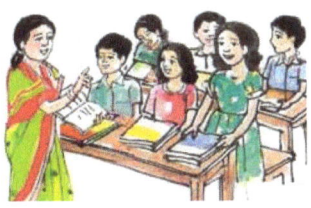

S1: Can we live well if we eat good food only, teacher?

T: No, you can't. You should do other things, too.

S2: What else should we do, teacher?

T : You should follow some rules.

S3: What are these rules, teacher?

T : These are:

You must

1☐ brush your teeth after meals.

2☐ cut your nails every week and keep them clean.

3☐ wash your hands with soap before meals and after using the toilet.

4☐ drink enough clean water.

A Read the questions and try to answer them.

1 Where does a bird live?
2 What is a cornfield? Where can you see a cornfield?
3 What does a bird do in a cornfield?

B Listen to the story and answer the questions that follow.

There is a cornfield. A bird with her little children lives there. The children are very young. They cannot fly yet. Every morning the mother bird flies off to find food for her children.

1 *Why does the mother bird fly off every morning?*

It is summer. The corn is ripe. One morning the mother says, "Children, the farmer may come into the field today. Listen to what he says. Tell me when I come back."

2 *What may happen when the corn is ripe?*

The mother comes back in the evening. The children say to her, " Mother, we must go away today. The farmer and his son came. They talked. The farmer is going to cut the corn tomorrow. The farmer's brothers will help him."

78

" Don't worry, children. His brothers have their own corn to cut. So we have enough time to wait."

3   *How do the children know that the farmer is going to cut his corn the next day?*

The next day the farmer and his son come and talk again. The mother returns in the evening and the children tell her, " Mother, the farmer will cut his corn tomorrow. This time his friends will help him."

" Don't worry children," says the mother. " His friends too have their own corn to cut."

4   *What will happen the next day?*

The next day the farmer and his son come and talk again. The children tell their mother, " The farmer is not going to wait for his brothers and friends. The corn is very ripe. He and his son will cut the corn themselves." The mother then says, " Now it's time for us to leave the cornfield."

5   *What will happen to the bird and her children if they wait longer?*

The End

Academic year 2013, English-3

Health is Wealth

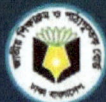

NATIONAL CURRICULUM & TEXTBOOK BOARD, DHAKA

www.ingramcontent.com/pod-product-compliance
Lightning Source LLC
Chambersburg PA
CBHW040820200526
45159CB00024B/3083